Stark County District Library
www.StarkLibrary.org
330.452.0665

FEB - - 2015

Y0-CJG-890

Pet Corner

TERRIFIC TURTLES

By Rose Carraway

Please visit our website, www.garethstevens.com. For a free color catalog of all our high-quality books, call toll free 1-800-542-2595 or fax 1-877-542-2596.

Library of Congress Cataloging-in-Publication Data

Carraway, Rose.
Terrific turtles / Rose Carraway.
    p. cm. — (Pet corner)
ISBN 978-1-4339-6311-7 (pbk.)
ISBN 978-1-4339-6312-4 (6-pack)
ISBN 978-1-4339-6309-4 (library binding)
1. Turtles as pets—Juvenile literature. I. Title.
SF459.T8C366 2012
639.3'92—dc23
                            2011024747

First Edition

Published in 2012 by
Gareth Stevens Publishing
111 East 14th Street, Suite 349
New York, NY 10003

Copyright © 2012 Gareth Stevens Publishing

Editor: Katie Kawa
Designer: Andrea Davison-Bartolotta

Photo credits: Cover, pp. 1, 7, 9, 11, 15, 19, 21 (food), 23, 24 (shell) Shutterstock.com; pp. 5, 21 (main) iStockphoto/Thinkstock; pp. 13, 24 (pen) iStockPhoto.com; pp. 17, 24 (tank) ballyscanlon/Photonica/Getty Images.

All rights reserved. No part of this book may be reproduced in any form without permission in writing from the publisher, except by a reviewer.

Printed in the United States of America

CPSIA compliance information: Batch #CW12GS: For further information contact Gareth Stevens, New York, New York at 1-800-542-2595.

Contents

A Hiding Place. 4

Where Turtles Live 10

Time to Eat 18

Words to Know 24

Index. 24

Turtles make cool pets!

A turtle can hide in its shell.

Its head, legs, and feet go inside.

One kind of pet turtle
is an aquatic turtle.
It lives in water.

Some pet turtles
live outside.
They live in a pen.

They sleep all winter.
This is called hibernating.

Some pet turtles
live inside.
They live in glass tanks.

Turtles eat many things.
They like fish.

They eat sticks
of turtle food, too.

21

Turtles can live
for a long time.
Some are 100 years old!

Words to Know

pen

shell

tank

Index

eat 18, 20

pen 12

tanks 16

water 10